BORDEAUX Travel Guide

Bordeaux Uncorked: A Traveler's Guide to French Elegance

COPYRIGHT

No part of this book may be reproduced, distributed, or transmitted in any form or by any means, including photocopying, recording, or other electronic or mechanical methods, without the prior written permission of the publisher, except in the case of brief quotations embodied in critical reviews and certain other non-commercial uses permitted by copyright law.

© [2025] [Evelina J.G.]
All rights reserved.

PREFACE

Greetings from the Bordeaux Travel Guide 2025, your all-in-one resource for learning about the allure of Bordeaux and its neighboring gems. Bordeaux, one of the most well-known travel destinations in France, is a must-see for tourists looking for life-changing experiences since it offers a unique fusion of culture, history, and contemporary elegance.

This book has been carefully crafted to provide you all the information you need to confidently and enthusiastically explore Bordeaux. This book will inspire and educate your travel, regardless of whether you are drawn to the city's architectural grandeur, its thriving culinary scene, or its world-class wines. Bordeaux offers breathtaking views at every turn, from the Old Town's cobblestone alleyways to the expansive vineyards that yield some of the world's best wines.

To ensure that it is a reliable resource and a source of inspiration, we have balanced pragmatism and passion in the creation of this handbook. Its pages contain well planned itineraries, expert advice, and comprehensive cultural insights. We've also celebrated Bordeaux's dedication to conserving its natural beauty for coming generations by highlighting eco-friendly travel strategies.

This book encourages you to experience Bordeaux to the fullest, regardless of your level of experience. Imagine enjoying a freshly baked canelé in a little café, riding a bicycle along the Garonne's banks, or sipping a glass of Saint-Émilion while the sun sets over the vineyards. Every chapter aims to ignite your creativity and provide you with the means to turn these visions into reality.

As you go out on this adventure, keep in mind that Bordeaux is an experience rather than merely a location. It's the connections made with the people who live in this amazing area, the wonder experienced when taking in centuries-old buildings, and the laughs shared over a delectable dinner.

Make this guide your ticket to Bordeaux's center. I hope it inspires you to venture out, delight your senses, and make memories that you will cherish long after you have returned home. Good luck on your journey!

TABLE OF CONTENTS

COPYRIGHT	2
PREFACE	3
TABLE OF CONTENTS	5
OVERVIEW	6
PLANNING YOUR TRIP	12
ACCOMMODATIONS	19
EXPLORATION	26
THE GLOBAL WINE CAPITAL	33
CULINARY EXPERIENCES	40
ARTS AND CULTURE	46
DAY TRIPS	52
ADVENTURES AND OUTDOOR ACTIVITIES	57
SHOPPING	64
SUSTAINABLE TRAVEL	71
USEFUL INFORMATION	79
BORDEAUX FOR DIFFERENT TRAVELERS	86
SEASONAL HIGHLIGHTS	94
FINAL TIPS AND INSIGHTS	101
APPENDIX	109

OVERVIEW

Bordeaux, a city in southwest France that is tucked away along the banks of the Garonne River, skillfully combines modern elegance with old-world beauty. Known as the world's wine center, this UNESCO World Heritage Site is known for its renowned vineyards as well as its vibrant cultural scene, fine dining, and stunning architecture. The city of Bordeaux, sometimes referred to as the "Pearl of Aquitaine," welcomes you to appreciate its history, beauty, and way of life at every opportunity.

Explore the ancient alleys of Saint-Pierre, the historic center of Bordeaux, or stroll along its graceful alleyways dotted with neoclassical houses. The ambiance here is rich in history, with cobblestones resonating with tales of bygone eras. Bordeaux, however, is a city that looks to the future rather than merely the past. Bordeaux has welcomed innovation without losing its core, as evidenced by its dedication to sustainability and the elegant, contemporary lines of La Cité du Vin.

Whether you're a wine connoisseur, a history buff, a foodie, or simply a tourist seeking an unforgettable vacation, Bordeaux offers a tapestry of activities that caters to every interest. From the tranquil beauty of the Garonne coastline to the dynamic hum of its busy markets, Bordeaux is a city that guarantees to captivate your heart and leave you craving for more.

The Reasons for Traveling to Bordeaux in 2025, Bordeaux continues to shine on the international scene with events, innovations, and opportunities that make it a must-see location, making 2025 a remarkable moment to visit. Bordeaux should be at the top of your list of places to visit.

The Pinnacle of Wine Tourism:
Although Bordeaux's vineyards have long been renowned, a number of improved and innovative wine experiences will be available in 2025. Visitors can learn more about the craft and history of winemaking as vintners offer their châteaux for immersive tours and tastings. One of the most prestigious wine festivals in the world, the Bordeaux Wine Festival, will return with its unmatched

celebration of legacy, craftsmanship, and flavors.

Cultural Significant Events:
Bordeaux's rich legacy and inventive spirit will be showcased through a variety of cultural festivals, exhibitions, and performances in 2025. The city's dynamic culture will be on full display, from live performances along the quays to state-of-the-art art exhibits at the CAPC Museum of Contemporary Art.

Utilizing Sustainability:
Bordeaux is regarded as one of the most sustainable towns in Europe because of its embracing of a greener future. Eco-friendly transportation choices, like a wider network of bike lanes and pedestrian zones, allow tourists to easily and sustainably explore the city. Its standing as an example of sustainable urban life will be further enhanced by new green projects in 2025.

Adventure Gateway:
Bordeaux is the ideal starting point for touring southwest France because of its ideal location. Beyond the city boundaries lies an adventure, whether it's a trek up the majestic Dune of Pilat, a beach getaway to Arcachon Bay, or a

day trip to the medieval beauty of Saint-Émilion.

Bordeaux in 2025 aspires to be more than just a vacation destination; it's a destination full of remarkable events, booming innovation, and timeless charm.

Essentials and Fast Facts
Here are some important details to help you organize your journey before you leave for Bordeaux:

Population: Approximately 260,000 in the city itself, plus around 800,000 in the metropolitan area. Bordeaux retains its small-town charm despite its size.

Language: Although English is widely spoken by locals working in the tourism and hospitality sectors, French is the official language. Your experience will be much improved by knowing a few simple French phrases.

The Euro (€) is the currency used. Although most places accept credit and debit cards, it's still a good idea to have some cash on hand for smaller businesses and markets.

Climate: The climate of Bordeaux is mild and oceanic. The warm, sunny summers are wonderful for touring vineyards, while the cool, rainy winters are perfect for sipping a glass of Bordeaux wine while relaxing in a quaint café.

The time zone is UTC+1, or Central European Time (CET). It changes to Central European Summer Time (CEST), UTC+2, during daylight saving time.

Moving Around: Trams, buses, and bike rentals are all part of Bordeaux's well-functioning public transportation network. It is simple to explore the city center on foot because it is small and pedestrian-friendly.

Foods You Must Try: Bordeaux is a culinary wonderland. Famous dishes like canelés (sweet custard pastries), oysters from neighboring Arcachon Bay, and entrecôte à la Bordelaise (rib steak with wine sauce) are not to be missed.

The Place de la Bourse & Miroir d'Eau, Bordeaux's famous square and reflecting water feature, is one of the city's top attractions.
- La Cité du Vin: A museum and cultural center dedicated to wine.

- Jardin Public: A quiet park in the center of the city.

One of the longest pedestrian shopping avenues in Europe is Rue Sainte-Catherine.

- Pont de Pierre: A graceful stone bridge with lovely Garonne views.

Trip Advice: Bordeaux can be explored on foot, but don't pass up the opportunity to see it from the water. A river cruise provides a distinctive viewpoint of the city's vibrant quays and breathtaking architecture.

Bordeaux is prepared to welcome you to an amazing journey in 2025 with its ideal fusion of history, innovation, and joie de vivre. Prepare to be engrossed in a city that will inspire you and stimulate your senses.

PLANNING YOUR TRIP

Bordeaux is conveniently accessible from major European cities and beyond due to its central location in southwest France. There are dependable and practical options to fit the needs of every traveler, whether they choose to drive, fly, or take the train. Here's a thorough look at how to get to this magical city.

By Air: Bordeaux-Mérignac Airport

Bordeaux-Mérignac Airport (BOD) serves as the primary gateway for travelers arriving by air. Located just 12 kilometers (7.5 miles) west of the city center, the airport is well-connected to numerous international and domestic destinations.

Airlines and Destinations:
The airport hosts a wide range of airlines, including major carriers like Air France, British Airways, and Lufthansa, as well as low-cost options such as Ryanair and easyJet. Flights from European centers including London, Paris, Amsterdam, and Madrid are frequent and convenient. In 2025, extended routes are projected to connect Bordeaux with additional

destinations, making it even easier to plan your journey.

Transportation from the Airport: Getting to the city center from the airport is straightforward:
- Bus: The Lianes 1+ bus service offers a cheap and reliable connection between the airport and Bordeaux's Gare Saint-Jean train station, with stops in the city center along the way.
- Airport Shuttle: The Navette Aéroport express shuttle provides direct access to central Bordeaux in roughly 30 minutes.
- Taxi and ridesharing: Taxis and ridesharing services like Uber are commonly available, with journey durations ranging from 20 to 40 minutes depending on traffic.
- Car Rental: For those wishing to visit the neighboring wine regions, hiring a car at the airport is a simple choice. Major car rental agencies have offices on-site.

By Train: High-Speed Rail Options

Bordeaux's Gare Saint-Jean is a significant hub in France's high-speed rail (TGV) network, making train travel one of the most efficient and eco-friendly methods to reach the city.

From Paris:
The TGV InOui provides a smooth and comfortable ride from Paris to Bordeaux in just over two hours. Trains depart frequently from Paris Montparnasse station, ensuring flexibility for travelers.

From Other Cities:
Additionally, Bordeaux has regional and high-speed rail connections to Lyon, Marseille, Toulouse, and Nantes. Renfe's cross-border services and SNCF offer international connections from Spain.

At the Station: Gare Saint-Jean is equipped with amenities including food options, luggage storage, and rental car services. The station is just a short tram or bus journey from Bordeaux's city center, ensuring simple onward travel.

By Road: Options for Driving and Buses

For those who prefer the flexibility of road travel, Bordeaux is well-connected by a network of highways and intercity bus routes.

Driving to Bordeaux:
Bordeaux is connected to other cities and regions by major highways:
Take the A10 from Paris; it's a beautiful journey that takes around six hours.

- From Toulouse, the A62 offers a direct route, with a travel time of roughly two and a half hours. - Bordeaux is the perfect option for travelers traveling abroad because the A63 connects it to both Spain and the Basque Country.

Once in Bordeaux, tourists should be aware that there aren't many parking spaces and the city center is mostly pedestrianized. To explore the city, think about parking at approved lots or garages on the outskirts and taking public transportation.

Bus Travel: Compared to driving, intercity bus services are more affordable. Frequent services to Bordeaux are offered by operators such as Ouibus, BlaBlaBus, and FlixBus from cities throughout France and Europe. Modern buses are a cost-effective option because they frequently provide power outlets, Wi-Fi, and comfortable seating, even though their trip times may be greater than those of trains.

Tips for Eco-Friendly Travel

Bordeaux promotes environmentally conscious tourism since it is a city dedicated to sustainability. The following advice will help you reduce your environmental effect while traveling to this exciting location:

1. Whenever feasible, take the train:
For medium-distance travel, high-speed trains are the most environmentally friendly choice because they generate substantially less CO_2 per passenger than cars or airplanes. Whenever possible, choose train lines, especially when traveling inside France and its surrounding nations.

2. Use Shared Transport Options: To lessen the number of cars on the road, think about carpooling or riding buses using services like BlaBlaCar. These choices are economical as well as environmentally beneficial.

3. Choosing Non-Stop Flights:
Select direct flights if you must fly in order to reduce the amount of fuel used for takeoffs and landings. It can also have an impact to support airlines that put sustainability first.

4. Eco-Friendly Car Rentals:
If hybrid or electric vehicles are available, choose these while renting a car. Bordeaux has a lot of rental companies that provide environmentally friendly cars, and the city has electric car charging points.

5. Light Pack:
Fuel usage in all forms of transportation is decreased by lighter luggage. Effective packing not only benefits the environment but also makes traveling easier.

6. Offset Your Carbon Footprint: To offset the emissions caused by your trip, think about buying carbon offsets. These days, a lot of airlines and travel agencies include this choice in the reservation process.

You may travel guilt-free and contribute to preserving Bordeaux's natural beauty for future generations by implementing these sustainable habits into your trip.

Arriving in Bordeaux is just as much of an adventure as touring the city. Reaching this captivating location has never been simpler or more fulfilling thanks to effective air, rail, and road connections as well as eco-friendly travel choices.

ACCOMMODATIONS

Bordeaux provides a large range of lodging options to suit every preference, price range, and mode of travel. There is accommodation for everyone, ranging from opulent hotels in the center of the city to quaint boutique guesthouses and reasonably priced hostels. Let's look at your possibilities because picking the correct neighborhood and lodging can make your trip much more enjoyable.

Top Communities

Every neighborhood in Bordeaux offers a variety of experiences and has its own distinct atmosphere. There is a neighborhood for everyone, whether you want to live surrounded by creative energy, immersed in history, or searching for a base that is affordable.

Le Vieux Bordeaux, Historic City Center)
The Historic City Center is the place to go if you want to be right in the middle of the activity. Famous sites including the Place de la Bourse, the Miroir d'Eau, and the busy Rue Sainte-Catherine can be found in this neighborhood, which is called Le Vieux

Bordeaux. The greatest eateries, retail establishments, and cultural sites in Bordeaux are all conveniently close by if you choose to stay here.

With its pedestrian-friendly streets and architectural treasures around every corner, the Historic City Center is the perfect place for people who enjoy exploring on foot. Accommodations range from opulent hotels set in historic structures to quaint guest houses with contemporary conveniences.

Artistic Charm: Chartrons
For a more relaxed and creative atmosphere, think about Chartrons. This neighborhood, which was formerly the center of Bordeaux's wine trade, is now a hip neighborhood with lots of art galleries, vintage stores, and quaint cafes. For tourists looking for a more sedate stay without venturing too far from the city center, it's ideal.

Additionally, Chartrons provides a range of lodging choices, from chic boutique hotels to roomy flats. The district's weekend markets are a must-see, and the riverfront promenade is a great place for morning strolls.

Saint-Michel: Inexpensive Locations
Saint-Michel is a great option if you're on a tight budget. Budget hotels and hostels are among the reasonably priced overnight alternatives available in this lively and ethnic neighborhood without sacrificing atmosphere.

Saint-Michel is well-known for the beautiful Basilica of Saint-Michel, its vibrant markets, and its diverse culinary options. It's a fantastic place to experience local culture and savor genuine Bordeaux without going over budget.

Types of Accommodations

Bordeaux offers a range of accommodations to suit all types of tourists, from luxurious hotels to affordable hostels. What to anticipate is as follows:

Hotels of Luxury
Bordeaux offers a remarkable array of opulent lodging options for individuals who appreciate the finest things in life. These include hotels with a global reputation and boutique establishments that offer outstanding service and elegance. The Historic City Center is home to a number of upscale hotels with features

including Michelin-starred restaurants, rooftop patios, and spa treatments.

Top Selections:
The magnificent five-star InterContinental Bordeaux Le Grand Hôtel offers views of the Opéra National.
The Hôtel de Sèze is well-known for its elegant furnishings and handy location.

Guesthouse Boutiques
The boutique guesthouses in Bordeaux are a great choice if you want a more private and distinctive stay. With their individualized touches and attentive hosts, these lodgings frequently capture the essence of the city's particular charm and personality.

Top Selections:
La Maison Bord'Eaux is a quaint guesthouse that combines modern and traditional design elements.
Situated in the center of the city, the L'Hotel Particulier offers chic accommodations in a welcoming setting.

Hostels and Budget Options
In Bordeaux, comfort does not have to be sacrificed for affordable travel. The city offers a

variety of reasonably priced lodging choices, including shared apartments, hostels, and low-cost hotels. Since many are situated in thriving areas like Saint-Michel, it's simple to take in the excitement of the city without going over budget.

Top Selections:
A welcoming and comfortable choice in the Chartrons neighborhood is Hostel 20 Bordeaux.
The Ibis Budget Bordeaux Centre offers dependable and reasonably priced lodging near major attractions.

Advice for Making Reservations

Choosing the ideal lodging in Bordeaux might improve your trip, so follow these helpful pointers to make sure everything goes smoothly:

1. Make reservations in advance:
Bordeaux is a well-liked vacation spot, particularly in the summer and during the Bordeaux Wine Festival. You may choose from more options and get better deals if you book your stay well in advance.

2. Take Public Transportation Nearby into Account:
Bordeaux is a pedestrian-friendly city, but it can be more convenient to explore the city and neighboring areas if you stay close to a tram or bus route.

3. Search for Packages and Offers:
Special packages that include extras like wine tastings, breakfast, or guided excursions are available at many hotels. To find out whether there are any specials going on, visit their websites or get in touch with them directly.

4. Set Amenities in Order of Priority: Consider what matters to you while visiting. Do you want lodgings that allow pets, on-site restaurants, or a pool? To fit your preferences, narrow down your search.

5. Examine Reviews:
Examining customer evaluations on websites such as Booking.com or TripAdvisor can give you important information about the caliber of the lodging and amenities offered.

6. Maintain Adaptability:
If your travel schedule is flexible, think about going in the spring or fall, when costs are lower and the city is less busy.

7. Examine Other Choices:
Websites like Airbnb and VRBO provide distinctive lodging options, including loft apartments or rural hideaways, that might enhance your trip to Bordeaux.

Selecting the ideal neighborhood and type of lodging will make your time in Bordeaux as delightful as the activities that await you outside. Bordeaux offers a variety of housing alternatives to guarantee a pleasant and unforgettable stay, regardless of your travel budget or preference for luxury.

EXPLORATION

The city of Bordeaux cries out for exploration. It provides excitement for every traveler with its mix of modern attractions, historic sites, and quaint streets. There's always something new to find in this energetic city, whether you like guided tours or finding hidden treasures.

Experiences and Tours with Guides

One of the greatest ways to see Bordeaux's rich history and culture is to go on a guided tour. From its medieval beginnings to its current position as a wine capital, knowledgeable guides enliven the city with tales that take you back in time.

Walking Tours: With the help of informed interpreters, tour Bordeaux's UNESCO-listed Historic City Center, passing by famous locations like the Place de la Bourse, the Grosse Cloche, and Rue Sainte-Catherine. A lot of excursions have a theme, with subjects like the history of Bordeaux wine, notable buildings, or even eerie stories.

Wine Tours: Bordeaux has earned its status as the wine capital of the world. Attend local vineyards in areas like Médoc, Saint-Émilion, and Graves as part of a wine-tasting trip. Winemaking customs and pairings with regional specialties are frequently included in guided tastings.

River Cruises: Take a sail down the Garonne River to see Bordeaux from a different angle. Short sightseeing excursions and opulent dinner cruises that highlight the city's lit skyline are among the available options.

Tours by bicycle: Cycling tours are an enjoyable and environmentally responsible option for energetic tourists to see the city. Numerous pathways lead you through Bordeaux's less well-known neighborhoods or along the picturesque riverbank.

Major Attractions and Landmarks

Without seeing Bordeaux's famous sites and landmarks, a trip there wouldn't be complete. The spirit and charm of the city are encapsulated in these highlights.

Location of the Bourse and the Eau Mirror

The Place de la Bourse is a masterpiece of 18th-century architecture and is arguably Bordeaux's most famous landmark. The city's historical wealth and prominence are reflected in this graceful square, which is surrounded by imposing buildings.

The largest reflecting pool in the world, the Miroir d'Eau, is located just across from the square. The pool is exquisitely lit at night and produces a captivating mirror effect of the surrounding architecture on sunny days. Don't pass up the opportunity to take pictures or just take in the peaceful atmosphere.

La Cité du Vin

Both wine lovers and inquisitive tourists should make time to visit La Cité du Vin. Through interactive exhibits, sensory encounters, and tastings, this futuristic cultural center honors wine's significance on a worldwide scale. The structure itself is a work of architectural art, modeled after the swirl of wine in a glass.

Visit the eighth-floor Belvedere for sweeping views of Bordeaux, which go well with the complimentary wine sampling.

Cathedral of Bordeaux
Cathédrale Saint-André, another name for Bordeaux Cathedral, is a magnificent example of Gothic architecture. Throughout Bordeaux's history, important occasions and royal marriages have taken place at this historic location.

For stunning city views, ascend the Pey-Berland Tower, which is next to the cathedral. Climbing the tower is a worthwhile effort that provides a fresh view of Bordeaux's skyline.

Off-the-Beaten-Path Locations and Hidden Gems

Bordeaux has many hidden gems just waiting to be found, even beyond the well-known sights. You should include the following off-the-beaten-path locations in your itinerary:

Public Jardin: This peaceful park in the middle of the city is ideal for a picnic or a leisurely walk. The Musée d'Histoire Naturelle, an intriguing destination for nature enthusiasts, is also located there.

This is the Darwin Ecosystem: This former military barracks on the Right Bank has been converted into a center for the arts. It has co-working spaces, eco-friendly eateries, and urban art. For those who love photography, the street art here is a delight.

Floating Bassins: Explore the nautical history of Bordeaux at this restored dockland. Highlights include Les Halles de Bacalan, a bustling food market, and the Submarine Base, which is now an immersive art space.

As stated by Pont de Pierre: With breathtaking views of the city skyline and the Garonne River, this medieval bridge is ideal for a leisurely bike ride or stroll.

Recommended Paths for Walking

Because of its small size and pedestrian-friendly streets, Bordeaux is a city that is best visited on foot. The following recommended walking routes will help you plan your adventures:

Historic Highlights go: - Commence at Place de la Bourse and go to the Miroir d'Eau along the riverbank.
- Visit one of France's oldest belfries, the Grosse Cloche.
- Take a moment to climb the Pey-Berland Tower before finishing your stroll at Bordeaux Cathedral.

Chartrons and Riverside Stroll: - Start by touring the antique stores and art galleries in Chartrons. Take in the sights of the Garonne River as you stroll down the Quai des Chartrons. For a gastronomic and cultural experience, visit La Cité du Vin.

Hidden Gems Trail: - Explore the lively areas of Darwin Ecosystème on the Right Bank first.
To unwind in Jardin Public, cross the Pont de Pierre to the Left Bank.
- Visit Les Bassins à Flot to round up your stroll.

Bordeaux is a city that encourages exploration and provides a wide range of activities for all kinds of tourists. The trip promises to be just as memorable as the final destination, whether you're exploring its hidden gems, discovering its famous landmarks, or just strolling down its quaint streets.

THE GLOBAL WINE CAPITAL

Bordeaux is a word that conjures up pictures of expansive vineyards, old châteaux, and glasses filled with some of the best vintages in the world. The region is synonymous with wine. Bordeaux, the world's heartland of winemaking, provides a multitude of activities for both oenophiles and inquisitive tourists. Discovering Bordeaux's wine culture is just as fascinating as the wines themselves, whether you're sipping wine in a sun-dappled vineyard or learning about centuries-old winemaking customs.

The History of Winemaking in Bordeaux

The history of Bordeaux wine dates back about two thousand years, to the time when the Romans established vineyards in the area circa 60 BCE. Bordeaux became an attractive place for viticulture very rapidly because of its distinctive terroir, which is a harmonious combination of temperature, soil, and topography. Bordeaux's fame expanded throughout time thanks to its advantageous location along the Garonne River, which made it simple to export to hungry consumers in the Netherlands, England, and other countries.

In the 12th century, a flourishing Bordeaux wine trade was cultivated by Eleanor of Aquitaine's marriage to Henry II of England. As the world's wine center by the 18th century, Bordeaux's reputation was further solidified by prestigious classifications such as the 1855 Bordeaux Wine Official Classification.

Bordeaux continues its history today, with more than 6,000 winemakers producing a wide range of wines, from bold reds to delicate whites and sweet dessert wines. Examining this extensive past gives each glass you sip in the area more depth.

Best Vineyards and Wineries to See

Bordeaux is home to a staggering array of vineyards and wineries, each with its own distinct viewpoint on winemaking. The following are some noteworthy locations:

Margaux Château
The Médoc region is home to Château Margaux, one of Bordeaux's most famous estates. Known for its sophisticated and

age-worthy wines, a trip here is like entering a timeless work of art. A tour of the vineyards, a look into the cellar, and a taste of their famous Grand Vin are all common features of guided tours.

Château Pape Clément
With a 14th-century winemaking heritage, this historic estate is part of the Pessac-Léognan appellation. Visitors can taste some of its outstanding wines while exploring its gorgeous grounds, modern winery, and ambiance-filled barrel chambers.

The Château d'Yquem
Sauternes' Château d'Yquem is a must-see for fans of sweet wines. Renowned for creating the best dessert wines in the world, a visit here provides a close-up view of the painstaking process that goes into making these golden concoctions.

Saint-Émilion Vineyards
A haven of medieval charm and viticultural brilliance, Saint-Émilion's vineyards are a UNESCO World Heritage Site. Unmatched experiences may be had in this charming area at wineries like Château Ausone and Château Cheval Blanc.

Wine Tastings and Tours

In order to really experience Bordeaux's wine culture, a guided wine tour is essential. Inaccessible châteaux can be accessed behind the scenes with the help of many tours, which also provide transportation and knowledgeable guides.

Personalized Encounters: Choose private tours based on your preferences, such as a crisp Sauvignon Blanc or a robust Cabernet Sauvignon. In order to provide breathtaking aerial views of Bordeaux's vineyards, some operators even set up helicopter tours.

Workshops for Blending: Making your own Bordeaux blend will allow you to take on the role of a winemaker. A practical way to comprehend the artistry behind Bordeaux's renowned blends is through workshops like those at Château Pape Clément or La Cité du Vin.

Pairing Wine and Food: Bordeaux's wines are the ideal match for its gastronomic scene. Numerous wineries offer gourmet experiences where you can enjoy regional cuisine and expertly matched wines.

Activities and Celebrations: Make sure to schedule your trip around Bordeaux's yearly wine festivals, like the Bordeaux Fête le Vin. To celebrate the best vintages in the area, these gatherings bring together wine lovers from all over the world.

Buying Advice for Bordeaux Wines

Buying Bordeaux wines is a skill unto itself. To make the most of your wine-buying experience, consider the following helpful advice:

1. Recognize Labels: Despite their complexity, Bordeaux wine labels are jam-packed with helpful information. Learn about appellation names like Margaux, Pauillac, or Graves, as well as terms like "Château," "Grand Cru," and others.

2. Establish a Budget: The Bordeaux wine line includes both investment-worthy collectibles and reasonably priced everyday bottles. Choose your spending limit beforehand, and don't be afraid to request suggestions that fit it.

3. **Purchase Straight from Wineries:** In addition to letting you sample before you buy, a château visit guarantees that you're getting genuine bottles at affordable costs. Even rare vintages that aren't available anywhere else are offered by some wineries.

4. **Consult a Professional:** Bordeaux is home to a large number of wine shops, or cavistes, with friendly staff who can help you choose what you like. Seek out stores with a large assortment and knowledgeable sommeliers.

5. **Take Shipping Options Into Account:** Many wineries and wine shops offer international shipping if you're buying large quantities of bottles or larger formats. Make sure to ask about the customs laws in your nation of origin.

6. **Investigate Little-Known Names:** Even though Médoc and Saint-Émilion are well-known, tasting wines from lesser-known appellations like Fronsac or Côtes de Bourg can produce interesting and more reasonably priced discoveries.

Bordeaux's wines reflect centuries of tradition, passion, and artistry and are more than just a drink. The experiences you have in Bordeaux, from strolling through sun-drenched vineyards to sipping Grand Cru vintages in historic cellars, will enhance your understanding of this world wine capital. I wish you luck as you explore Bordeaux's wine treasures!

CULINARY EXPERIENCES

Every dish in Bordeaux's culinary scene conveys a tale of passion, creativity, and tradition, making it a feast for the senses. From upscale restaurants to vibrant food markets, the city welcomes you to enjoy cuisines as diverse as its past. Every dish and drink here transports you to the heart of French cuisine, making Bordeaux a must-see location for foodies.

Must-Try Classic Bordeaux Recipes

The best way to understand Bordeaux is to begin with its famous cuisine. The region's superb local products and traditional methods are showcased in these culinary gems:

The dish "Entrecôte à la Bordelaise" honors Bordeaux's winemaking legacy by serving a perfectly cooked, juicy rib steak with a red wine and shallot sauce.
Canelé: Bordeaux is symbolized by this little pastry with a soft custard middle and caramelized edges. It has an enticingly rich flavor of rum and vanilla.

Arcachon Bay's fresh and briny oysters are a local delicacy and are frequently served with a crisp white Bordeaux wine.
Lamproie à la Bordelaise: A classic dish that consists of lamprey stewed in a robust red wine sauce that is seasoned with herbs and garlic.
- Foie Gras: An opulent treat, frequently served with sweet sides like sauternes wine or fig jam.

Top Cafés and Dining Establishments

From Michelin-starred restaurants to little neighborhood bistros, Bordeaux's culinary options appeal to all tastes.

Luxurious Dining Options

The book "Le Pressoir d'Argent" by Gordon Ramsay: With dishes that take regional flavors to the next level, this two-Michelin-starred restaurant in the Grand Hôtel de Bordeaux provides a sumptuous dining experience.

The Grand Maison de Bernard Magrez: World-renowned chefs create the wonderful delicacies served at this elegant location, which combines art and gastronomy.

Jan Ramet Restaurant: Located along the Garonne River, this restaurant offers exquisite food and breathtaking views of the waterfront.

Favorites from Locals

A local favorite for those looking for real flavors, Le Petit Commerce is renowned for its fresh fish and vibrant atmosphere.

A testament to its ongoing appeal, L'Entrecôte is a bistro that is well-known for its straightforward yet flawless steak frites. It frequently has lines out the door.

In a laid-back atmosphere, the lovely Café Anders is a great place to eat regional cuisine.

Vegetarian and Vegan Choices

Mangez Ça is a unique vegan restaurant that uses plant-based ingredients to recreate classic French cuisine.

- Wild Note Vegan Burger: Popular among both vegans and non-vegans, this laid-back restaurant is well-known for its delicious, substantial burgers.

Kitchen Garden: Fresh juices and organic vegetarian food are served at this quaint café.

Food Markets and Street Food

Discover the lively markets and street food options in Bordeaux to get a sense of its thriving culinary culture:

The vibrant market known as Bordeaux's "belly," the Marché des Capucins, is a great spot to try local cheeses, charcuterie, and fresh seafood. With a glass of white wine, don't overlook the oysters.

"Marché de Quais": cuisine trucks serving gourmet street cuisine, artisan crafts, and regional delicacies are all featured at this weekend market along the Garonne River.

Les Halles de Bacalan: Not far from La Cité du Vin, this contemporary food hall serves a carefully chosen assortment of regional goods and cuisine prepared by leading chefs.

Parades of Street Food: You may enjoy inventive tastes from all over the region by scheduling your visit around events like the Bordeaux Food Truck Festival.

Tours and Classes in Cooking

Increase your understanding of Bordeaux's cuisine through interactive activities and escorted tours:

- Cooking Classes: In small groups, talented chefs teach you how to make traditional Bordeaux meals. To provide students a true farm-to-table experience, many sessions involve field trips to nearby markets to choose fresh ingredients.
- Workshops on Wine and Cheese Pairing: Learn how to pair Bordeaux's best cheeses with its famous wines. Often, these sessions are held in charming wineries or cellars.
- Culinary Walking Tours: Take a knowledgeable guide on a stroll through Bordeaux's ancient districts, stopping along the way to taste foie gras, canelés, and other treats from artisan stores.

Experience Dining at the Château: Some wineries in Bordeaux provide private dining experiences where you may have fine dinner while taking in the grapes' splendor.

Taste, innovation, and tradition are all celebrated in Bordeaux's cuisine. Savor the city's unique culinary soul as each dish and dining experience tells a tale. Both your palate and your heart will be forever changed by your Bordeaux culinary adventure, from the first sip of wine to the last mouthful of canelé.

ARTS AND CULTURE

Bordeaux, a city known for its classic elegance, is a mosaic of rich cultural diversity and artistic expression. Its creative spirit permeates everything, from vivid street art to venerable museums. Every tourist can find something to inspire and enthrall them in Bordeaux's cultural landscape, regardless of whether they are a lover of live music or fine art. The city's arts sector is expected to be more active than before in 2025, beckoning you to take in its poetic beauty.

Galleries and Museums

With pieces spanning ages and genres, Bordeaux's museums and galleries offer a glimpse into the city's creative spirit. These establishments provide evidence of the city's unwavering dedication to creativity and culture.

Musée d'Art Contemporain CAPC

The CAPC Musée d'Art Contemporain, a mainstay of Bordeaux's modern art scene, is housed in a former warehouse. The avant-garde art it houses stands in stark juxtaposition to its industrial construction. The museum is a vibrant place where creativity thrives because of its changing exhibitions, which include pieces by both well-known and up-and-coming artists. Explore its expansive halls to find multimedia works, sculptures, and installations that subvert expectations and spark creativity.

Musée des Beaux-Arts

A wealth of European art may be seen at the Musée des Beaux-Arts, which is tucked away in the center of the city. With works by masters like Rubens, Delacroix, and Picasso, the collection covers the Renaissance to the 20th century. After viewing the museum's exhibits, the peaceful gardens offer the ideal place to unwind. A unique exhibition honoring the impact of Bordeaux's landscapes on French Impressionism is scheduled for the museum in 2025.

2025 Events and Festivals

Bordeaux's 2025 calendar is jam-packed with events honoring the city's creative legacy and modern inventiveness. Art and culture take center stage as the city is transformed into a living stage by these activities.

The International Art Fair in Bordeaux: Artists, collectors, and aficionados from all over the world come together for this yearly event. Anticipate cutting-edge installations and an emphasis on environmentally friendly artistic methods in 2025.

The Festival of Music: Bordeaux comes alive every June during its citywide music event. The festival honors the common language of music with everything from small musicians in secret courtyards to classical ensembles in opulent venues.

The Literary Escales: Writers, poets, and readers are invited to participate in readings, seminars, and debates that emphasize the transformational potential of words at this literary festival.

The Scene for Music and Theater

Stories are brought to life and melodies are profoundly felt in Bordeaux's theaters and music venues. The city's commitment to cultural enrichment and its lively artistic atmosphere are reflected in these areas.

Bordeaux's opera and ballet companies are housed in the Grand Théâtre de Bordeaux, a stunning example of neoclassical architecture. Its 2025 season promises to be a remarkable evening of grace and artistry, featuring both modern and old classics.
The Rocher de Palmer says: This multifaceted Cenon venue is a center for techno, jazz, and world music. There is always something to move the soul and thrill the ears thanks to its varied lineup.
- Comédie Gallien: For those who enjoy small-scale theater, this iconic space presents a selection of French and foreign plays that are thought-provoking, enjoyable, and inspirational.

Street Art in Bordeaux

Beyond its opulent theaters and galleries, Bordeaux's streets are blank canvases for colorful, provocative artwork. The city's receptiveness to contemporary artistic expression is demonstrated by its street art movement.

The Ecosystem of Darwin

The Darwin Ecosystem, a hub for street art and urban culture, is situated on the Right Bank. Its walls are covered in striking graffiti and murals that highlight the skills of both domestic and foreign artists. The vibrant setting, which combines elements of a cultural center and co-working space, making it an essential destination for fans of modern art.

Chatrons de Quartier

Discover a variety of street art that accentuates the artistic atmosphere of the Chartrons neighborhood as you stroll about it. Here, old buildings and vibrant murals coexist harmoniously, fostering a conversation between the past and present.

Annual Festival of Street Art

The Street Art Festival in Bordeaux turns public areas into galleries and offers classes and live painting sessions. A fantastic collection of artists is promised for the 2025 edition, whose inventive works will completely transform the urban landscape of the metropolis.

The artistic and cultural landscape of Bordeaux is a celebration of human ingenuity and expression. The city welcomes you to engage with its rich creative legacy, whether you're looking at a painting that dates back centuries or finding a hidden mural. In 2025, let the art of Bordeaux arouse your sense of surprise and inspire your spirit.

DAY TRIPS

Beyond Bordeaux lies a world of amazing day adventures, each with its own unique blend of adventure and charm. The surrounding area is full of places that offer life-changing experiences, whether you're a history buff, wine aficionado, or nature lover. All of these fascinating locations are easily accessible from the city, so pack your daypack and get ready to explore them.

A UNESCO Treasure: Saint-Émilion

The medieval village of Saint-Émilion, tucked away amid undulating vineyards, is a must-see for both history buffs and wine enthusiasts. The cobblestone lanes, historic buildings, and top-notch vineyards of this UNESCO World Heritage Site captivate tourists.

Take a guided tour of the Monolithic Church, a magnificent building carved out of limestone rock, to begin your adventure. For sweeping views of the surrounding vineyards, which appear to go on forever in the golden sunlight, climb the bell tower. Explore the quaint streets, where cafés and boutique stores beckon you to stay and take in the atmosphere.

A trip to Saint-Émilion wouldn't be complete without sampling some of its wines. Attend a tasting at a nearby château to discover more about the area's extensive winemaking history and to taste some of its well-known Merlot-dominant blends. You can gain a greater understanding of the trade by taking one of the many winery excursions that explore the science and art behind each bottle.

The Dune of Pilat and Arcachon Bay

Go west to Arcachon Bay for a cool beach getaway. This coastal hideaway is well-known for its serene waters, oyster farms, and the famous Dune of Pilat, the tallest sand dune in Europe.

Climb the Dune of Pilat to start your journey. With stunning views of the Atlantic Ocean on one side and verdant pine forests on the other, the climb is worthwhile. Take a minute to appreciate the breathtaking scenery and inhale the salty sea air at the top.

After that, visit some of the bay's quaint villages, such as Le Canon and L'Herbe, where you may have freshly shucked oysters with crisp white wine from the area. Take a boat cruise to see the bay's serene waters and its famous Île aux Oiseaux (Bird Island) for a distinctive viewpoint.

Arcachon town, with its upscale stores and beachfront eateries, is the perfect place to end your day. Savor seafood specialties while observing the sun set and the sky turn pink and orange.

Médoc and its Vineyards

The Médoc region, which is home to some of the best wines in the world, is only a short drive north of Bordeaux. Every sip reveals a tale of passion and tradition in this land of renowned labels and opulent châteaux.

Set out on a lovely excursion through vineyards interspersed with great estates along the Route des Châteaux. Discover the painstaking winemaking process with a guided tour at renowned wineries like Château Margaux or Château Pichon Baron. Admire these estates' magnificent architecture, which is a tribute to the area's rich history.

You can enjoy the robust Cabernet Sauvignon blends that characterize Médoc by attending one of the many châteaux that provide well planned tasting events. For a genuinely immersive experience, enjoy your wine with a fine picnic amidst the vines.

Beyond wine, the Médoc region has charming villages and peaceful bike routes that are ideal for leisurely exploration.

Cognac: An ebullient getaway

The town of Cognac, the birthplace of the renowned spirit, is farther away but well worth the trip. This quaint location blends a lively riverbank atmosphere, handmade workmanship, and a wealth of history.

Visit one of the main Cognac houses, such Hennessy, Rémy Martin, or Martell, to start your day. The complex process of making Cognac, from distillation to aging in oak barrels, is revealed on guided tours. You'll be able to sample many types and get an understanding of the subtleties that distinguish each brand.

Explore the medieval old town of Cognac, whose cobblestone streets and half-timbered homes give off an air of timeless elegance. A wonderful fusion of history and modernity can be seen in the Château de Cognac, a medieval stronghold converted into a Cognac distillery.

Enjoy a tranquil boat trip along the Charente River for a relaxed afternoon that provides breathtaking views of the town and its verdant surroundings. Enjoy a dinner at a riverfront cafe while there, sampling delicacies that go well with the area's distinctive personality.

The area around Bordeaux offers a wealth of experiences to suit a variety of interests. Every day trip offers a different combination of culture, adventure, and luxury, making your trip as varied as it is unforgettable. Your next journey can be inspired by the wine tradition of Médoc, the passionate heritage of Cognac, the maritime appeal of Arcachon, and the vineyards of Saint-Émilion.

ADVENTURES AND OUTDOOR ACTIVITIES

Bordeaux is a city that embraces nature and welcomes tourists to enjoy its splendor through a wide range of thrilling outdoor pursuits. Bordeaux is a haven for adventure seekers, whether they choose to cycle through verdant vineyards, cruise the magnificent Garonne River, or spend some peaceful time in the city's tranquil parks. As you appreciate the colorful scenery and the activities that lie ahead, let your curiosity run wild.

Bordeaux and Beyond riding Trails
Bordeaux is renowned for its bike-friendly environment and has a number of beautiful riding routes that meander through the city and into the surrounding countryside. It is ideal for cyclists of all skill levels, from novices to experts, due to its level terrain and clearly indicated routes.

Take a ride on the Garonne River to begin your journey. With kilometers of paved walkways connecting important parts of the city, the

Garonne riverbank has been turned into a cyclist's paradise. Take a refreshing break at one of the quaint riverfront cafés or pedal along the river's edge and observe the light reflecting off the water. The region next to the contemporary Bordeaux Bastide neighborhood is very charming, offering views of the famous Pont de Pierre and the old city center.

Consider riding through the renowned Médoc or Entre-deux-Mers wineries if you're looking for a more rustic getaway. In addition to producing some of the best wines in the world, these regions include bike paths that provide breathtaking views of undulating hills, charming towns, and vineyards that spread to the horizon. As you glide across the countryside, taking in the fresh air and the soft hum of nature, you'll feel as though you've entered a picture.

Many tour companies provide bicycle trips throughout Bordeaux, including vineyard tours where you may sample some of the best wines in the area while learning about the winemaking process, for those who would rather have a guided experience. Cycling is one of the greatest ways to experience Bordeaux's natural beauty and its environs at your own leisure, regardless of the route you take.

River Cruises and Boat Tours
A trip to Bordeaux wouldn't be complete without taking in the city's vitality, the Garonne River. With breathtaking views of the city's magnificent architecture and charming shoreline, a boat trip or river cruise is an excellent opportunity to experience Bordeaux from a different angle. The river offers something for everyone, regardless of your preference for an exciting boat ride or a relaxed cruise.

If you want to unwind, consider taking a leisurely river cruise through Bordeaux, which offers unhindered views of the city's ancient sites, like the Place de la Bourse and the stunning Quais de Bordeaux. Savor a bottle of Bordeaux wine while taking in the lively atmosphere of the city's riverbank and the soft air. Dinner is also included on some cruises, so you may savor delectable regional fare while taking in the sunset over the Garonne.

Consider renting a kayak or stand-up paddleboard if you want a more active experience. Navigate the serene river and discover the city's hidden gems as you glide across the water at your own speed. There's no better way to enjoy a full-body workout and connect with Bordeaux's marine heritage. See the striking architecture, paddle along the riverbanks, and maybe even spot some of the native fauna that calls the river home.

Take a boat tour down the Garonne that takes you outside of Bordeaux to explore neighboring attractions for a little more adventure. Embark on a river trip that heads out toward the Bassin d'Arcachon, a lovely natural harbor renowned for its oyster farms, sandy beaches, and breathtaking coastline. Alternatively, take a trip down the Garonne to see the quaint town of Langon, where you can take in the peace and quiet of the countryside and visit local wineries or markets.

Gardens & Parks
Bordeaux is a city of lush parks and lovely gardens that offer tranquil havens right in the middle of the city, in addition to its breathtaking architecture and mouth watering wine. Bordeaux's parks are ideal for outdoor enthusiasts who wish to get away from the bustle, whether they are looking for a spot to unwind, enjoy a picnic, or spend time in

nature. Let's examine two of the most cherished green areas in the city.

Public Garden
Nestled in the center of Bordeaux's Chartrons neighborhood, the Jardin Public is a peaceful haven that combines historical charm with scenic splendor. The park is ideal for a leisurely picnic or an afternoon stroll because of its large open areas, lovely flower beds, and serene pond.

Pause to admire the big chestnut trees that border the walks, the well-kept gardens, and the symmetry of the paths. With its many statues and sculptures, the park offers guests a chance to engage with Bordeaux's creative side. The park's tranquil mood is further enhanced by a quaint little lake where kids can feed ducks and swans as you stroll around.

The Bordeaux Natural History Museum, located in the Jardin Public, offers further information about the local flora and fauna for those who enjoy botanical gardens. The park is a great area for families to relax because it has playgrounds for those who are traveling with kids. The Jardin Public is a pleasant escape from the city, whether you're exploring the park's hidden corners or just relaxing by the pond.

Bordelais Park
The Parc Bordelais, which is situated in the lovely Caudéran neighborhood, is another treasure in Bordeaux's green areas. With its wide lawns, serene lakes, and meandering paths, this spacious park is the perfect place for a leisurely stroll or a peaceful afternoon in the great outdoors.

The park's tranquil lake, where guests can rent tiny boats and float leisurely across the water, is one of its most alluring features. The park's serene atmosphere is enhanced by the swaying reeds and weeping willows that surround you as you row along. There is also a beautiful pavilion in the park, which is ideal for picnics or a peaceful moment to unwind while taking in the lake view.

Parc Bordelais provides a variety of outdoor activities for those with a little more energy, including huge open spaces for sports and picnics as well as running and cycling pathways. Because the park is so well-liked by the people, you frequently see families, cyclists, and runners enjoying this verdant area. For anyone who wants to get away from the city and spend time in nature, this is the ideal location.

There are a ton of outdoor adventure options in Bordeaux. There is something for every adventurer, including leisurely boat rides down the Garonne, verdant parks for a peaceful getaway, and bike routes that lead you through the city and into the vineyard-covered countryside. Bordeaux is ready to show you the best of nature, history, and enjoyment, regardless of the outdoor activity you pick.

SHOPPING

Bordeaux is a sophisticated city that welcomes you to indulge in a little retail therapy in addition to being a destination for outstanding wine and cuisine. Bordeaux has something to fulfill every shopper's needs, whether they are looking for fine wine, exclusive crafts, or luxury apparel. Bordeaux's shopping environment is as stylish and varied as the city itself, with everything from hip boutiques to quaint artisan markets. So get ready to stroll around the chic streets and find the hidden gems in this chic French city.

Regional Handicrafts and Memorabilia
Numerous regional craftspeople in Bordeaux have honed their skills over many generations, producing a wide range of handcrafted artifacts that would make ideal presents or mementos. The Marché des Capucins, Bordeaux's biggest and liveliest market, is a great place to start your shopping journey because it offers a wide variety of locally made goods. The market is a visual feast and the ideal place to find one-of-a-kind mementos that capture the essence of the area, whether they be exquisitely

created jewelry, handmade soaps, or exquisitely designed home goods.

Visit Les Docks Cité de la Mode et du Design, a chic industrial structure that houses regional designers and artisans that combine traditional craftsmanship with modern flair, for something genuinely authentic. Unique apparel, accessories, and jewelry that capture Bordeaux's unique style can be found here. These homemade products, which range from custom leather purses to handwoven scarves, perfectly encapsulate Bordeaux's culture and inventive spirit.

Explore the Les Artisans de Bordeaux store, where regional artisans display their skills, if you're searching for something a little unusual. Treasures such as elaborately made pottery, embroidered linens, and hand-carved wooden artifacts can be found here. In addition to being exquisite, these objects also preserve the customs and tales of Bordeaux's artisan community, making them priceless keepsakes of your visit.

Boutiques and Wine Shops
Without taking in Bordeaux's renowned wine scene, a trip there would not be complete. With

a carefully chosen assortment of the best local and regional wines, Bordeaux is home to some of the greatest wine shops and boutiques. Bordeaux's wine shops promise a memorable shopping experience, regardless of your level of wine expertise or your desire to bring home a bottle or two.

La Cité du Vin, an architectural wonder devoted to the history, culture, and appreciation of wine, is the ideal place to begin your wine trip. Aside from being a museum and cultural hub, it also has a fantastic wine shop with a vast selection of Bordeaux wines from all across the area. You can choose the ideal bottle to take home or even to enjoy on your next wine tasting excursion with the assistance of the friendly staff.

Le Comptoir du Vin provides a carefully chosen selection of premium Bordeaux wines and rare labels for people looking for boutique experiences. The store's welcoming atmosphere makes it the ideal place to find limited-edition and rare bottles that aren't available in other stores. Inquire with the proprietor about the best wines to combine with your meals or peruse the vintage collection, which features a good representation of Bordeaux's esteemed wine estates.

The carefully chosen variety of premium wines at Maison du Vin de Bordeaux is ideal for wine enthusiasts looking for something exceptional. With a vast selection of Bordeaux wines ranging from well-known Grand Crus to up-and-coming boutique producers, this legendary boutique gives you the chance to take a bit of Bordeaux's winemaking heritage home with you.

Upscale Retail Avenues
Unquestionably sophisticated, Bordeaux's upscale retail avenues capture the city's elegant and international atmosphere. Discover the ideal fusion of high-end stores, designer boutiques, and globally recognized brands along Rue Sainte-Catherine, one of Europe's longest pedestrian avenues. Bordeaux's commercial sector is centered on this chic road, which sells everything from high-end clothing to fine accessories and cosmetics.

Visit Bordeaux's golden triangle of luxury shopping, Le Triangle d'Or, if you're looking for something genuinely unique. Some of Bordeaux's best high-end boutiques may be found here, tucked away between the classy Place des Grands Hommes and Place de la Bourse. A variety of high-end fashion houses can be found here, including global designers such as Gucci, Chanel, and Louis Vuitton, as well as stylish French labels that perfectly capture French flare and elegance.

The stunning architecture that envelops the Triangle will captivate you as you explore it. This posh neighborhood is an experience rather than merely a place to shop. For those looking for both luxury and style, the tree-lined roads, elegant façades, and lavish stores make this the ideal place to shop. Enjoy some luxury shopping, wander for a while, or just take in the atmosphere of Bordeaux's most renowned retail district.

Antique and Used Items
The range of possibilities offered by Bordeaux's vintage and second-hand stores is ideal for individuals who enjoy the excitement of finding unique treasures and hidden jewels. Bordeaux is a haven for vintage enthusiasts and treasure seekers, with its carefully curated second-hand boutiques and antique shops.

Begin your adventure with Le Marché aux Puces de Bordeaux, a large flea market that is ideal for discovering one-of-a-kind artwork, vintage apparel, antiques, and retro home décor. This lively market, which is just outside the city center, is a must-visit for anybody who enjoys nostalgia and finds hidden gems. While taking in the vibrant ambiance of this antique market, you can spend hours searching among unique artifacts, old music, and retro furniture.

Rendez-vous Vintage is a must-see for fashion enthusiasts. This stylish vintage shop has a well-chosen assortment of antique apparel and accessories, including classic Parisian styles, timeless designer pieces, and retro ensembles from earlier decades. Rendez-vous Vintage is a must-visit for everyone who appreciates all things fashionable and eco-friendly, regardless of whether they are searching for a statement piece to add to their wardrobe or are just interested in learning more about the world of vintage fashion.

An additional treasure is La Recyclerie Bordelaise, an environmentally conscious store that specializes in upcycled goods, furniture, and used clothing. The business sells a unique selection of gently used goods that are both sustainable and unique. For individuals who wish to find something genuinely unique while shopping ethically, La Recyclerie is the ideal place to find old leather coats and retro furniture.

Bordeaux offers a shopping experience that is as varied and rich as the city itself, skillfully fusing elegance, style, and inventiveness. Bordeaux welcomes you to discover and savor the better things in life, from world-class wineries and upscale fashion boutiques to regional crafts and handmade creations. You're sure to find something that embodies this stylish French city, whether you're searching for a bottle of Bordeaux's best wine to take home, an exclusive designer item, or a classic vintage treasure. Prepare to explore, shop, and enjoy everything Bordeaux has to offer.

SUSTAINABLE TRAVEL

Bordeaux, one of the most famous and stunning towns in France, is dedicated to protecting its environment and encouraging eco-friendly travel. Bordeaux provides a variety of options to lessen your environmental effect while still taking advantage of everything this energetic city has to offer, regardless of your level of experience with sustainable travel. The city is taking action to make sure that tourism benefits the environment and the local community by providing eco-friendly lodging and green transportation options. Here are some sustainable ways to enjoy Bordeaux.

Sustainable Accommodations
Bordeaux is home to an increasing number of eco-friendly hotels that prioritize sustainability while providing a comfortable stay. To lessen their impact on the environment, several of these hotels have implemented energy-saving strategies, employ organic and locally produced materials, and prioritize trash minimization.

Begin your stay in the opulent yet eco-friendly Hotel de Seze in the center of Bordeaux. With eco-friendly features including water-saving systems, energy-efficient lighting, and an emphasis on natural cleaning supplies, this boutique hotel is dedicated to sustainability. In addition to implementing sustainable procedures, the hotel places a strong emphasis on obtaining local cuisine in its restaurant, serving seasonal and organic dishes that showcase the city's dedication to quality and sustainability.

Mama Shelter Bordeaux is another choice for environmentally aware tourists; it is renowned for its green activities and contemporary design. The hotel is dedicated to cutting waste through recycling initiatives and avoiding single-use plastics, and it makes use of energy-efficient systems and sustainable building materials. It's a fantastic option for anyone who likes to have a fashionable and lively vacation while being conscious of their environmental effect.

With its use of sustainable toiletries and eco-friendly cleaning supplies, La Maison Bord'eaux provides a comfortable and eco-friendly setting for a more boutique experience. In order to ensure that a large portion of its furnishings and décor are sourced sustainably, the hotel also supports regional craftspeople. By booking accommodations like these, you're supporting environmentally friendly practices and directly boosting the local economy.

Eco-Friendly Transportation Choices
Bordeaux provides a range of eco-friendly transportation choices that reduce your carbon impact while making city navigation simple. Cycling is one of the most environmentally friendly ways to see Bordeaux. Because of the city's well-known bike lanes, riding a bike is a fun and convenient way to get around. You may easily rent a bike and tour the city at your own leisure thanks to the many bike rental services that are available, such as Vélo Bordeaux Métropole. In addition to lessening your environmental effect, cycling lets you take in Bordeaux's breathtaking scenery up close, from its medieval alleys to its picturesque riverbank.

Bordeaux's TBM (Transports Bordeaux Métropole) network offers a variety of environmentally responsible travel choices for individuals who like public transportation. Electricity powers the city's buses and trams, lowering emissions and dependency on fossil fuels. With connections to major tourist destinations including the Place de la Bourse,

Jardin Public, and Bordeaux's waterfront, the tram system is very practical for visitors. Using public transportation is not only a cost-effective method to get around the city, but it is also an environmentally conscious one.

Think about utilizing shared electric automobiles or electric scooters whether you're going within the city or to neighboring locations. These choices are a fantastic substitute for conventional taxis, enabling you to move around swiftly and effectively while reducing your carbon footprint. Electric scooter rentals are available from a number of businesses, and you can conveniently pick them up and leave them off at several spots throughout the city.

Last but not least, Bordeaux offers eco-friendly travel possibilities due to its close proximity to stunning natural settings. To lessen the environmental effect of your out-of-town travels, a number of nearby vineyards and wineries provide electric car rentals or guided tours.

Assisting Regional Companies
One of the most effective methods to travel sustainably in Bordeaux is to support local

companies. You can lessen the environmental costs of large production and long-distance shipping by buying locally produced goods, dining at restaurants that prioritize sustainable sourcing, and shopping at local markets.

Begin by seeing Bordeaux's Marché des Capucins, a bustling marketplace that sells a variety of organic products, handmade goods, and fresh, locally grown fruit. Buying products and food from nearby suppliers helps small-scale, sustainable agriculture and cuts down on food miles. Numerous market sellers place a high value on organic farming methods and seek to reduce their environmental impact.

Select dining establishments that use sustainable methods, such as promoting plant-based cuisine, limiting food waste, and sourcing foods locally. A great example is Le Chien de Pavlov, which serves food that emphasizes sustainable farming methods and locally sourced, seasonal ingredients. Another excellent choice is La Table de Pierre, a restaurant that collaborates closely with regional, environmentally concerned suppliers to serve farm-to-table cuisine.

There are also a lot of local stores in Bordeaux that provide handcrafted items created by craftspeople using eco-friendly materials. Think about going to stores like Les Docks Cité de la Mode et du Design, where regional designers and artisans provide goods that honor Bordeaux's distinctive culture while emphasizing environmental awareness.

You may help create a more sustainable economy and develop a greater understanding of Bordeaux's rich customs and regional craftsmanship by patronizing these companies.

Carbon Footprint Reduction Advice
While visiting Bordeaux, there are easy yet efficient ways to lessen your carbon footprint, and even minor adjustments can make a significant difference in your overall environmental impact. Here are some eco-friendly travel suggestions to remember while you're there:

1. Stay longer and travel less: Take your time exploring Bordeaux thoroughly rather than cramming yourself into a full schedule. Longer stays in one location cut down on the amount of transportation you need, which lowers carbon emissions.

2. Pack light: Lightening your luggage not only facilitates travel but also helps reduce emissions whether traveling by train or airplane.

3. Select eco-friendly gifts: Instead of mass-produced things, choose souvenirs that support local craftsmen or are manufactured from sustainable materials.

4. prevent single-use plastics: Bordeaux is dedicated to minimizing plastic waste, so when you visit, be sure to bring reusable shopping bags, coffee cups, and water bottles to prevent single-use plastics.

5. Eat sustainably: Since the cuisine of Bordeaux is focused on seasonal and local resources, choose plant-based and organic foods that are less harmful to the environment.

6. Reduce waste: Pay attention to waste during your journey, including packaging and meals. Make sure to properly dispose of your rubbish because Bordeaux has several recycling bins located across the city as part of its green initiatives.

Bordeaux is a stunning city that offers visitors a lively and sustainable experience while being dedicated to preserving its environment. There are numerous methods to travel sustainably and lessen your influence on the city's valuable resources, whether you're booking accommodations at eco-friendly hotels, using green transportation, patronizing neighborhood businesses, or just being aware of your everyday routine. You may fully enjoy Bordeaux and help create a more sustainable future by implementing some easy activities during your stay.

USEFUL INFORMATION

Making the most of your vacation to Bordeaux requires preparation, and planning a trip there is a fascinating journey. This section provides crucial, clear guidance to make sure your stay in Bordeaux is stress-free and enjoyable, from learning the basics of the language and currency to knowing what to do in an emergency. Here are some useful pointers to help you make the most of your visit.

Tips for Communication and Language
Although Bordeaux's official language is French, the city is used to foreign tourists, and many residents who work in the tourism sector know English to some degree. That being said, you may improve your experience and establish a connection with the local culture by learning a few simple French phrases. The following essential phrases will be useful:

"Bonjour (bohn-zhoor)" means "Hello."
Merci (mehr-see) - I'm grateful.
Please. - S'il vous plaît (seel voo pleh)
Please pardon me (ex-kew-zay mwah) and
Do you speak English? Are you able to communicate in English?

Where are you? Oo eh) - Where is... (helpful for instructions)

Although knowing the fundamentals of French is beneficial, patience and respect are essential for effective communication. Even a simple "hello" or "thank you" is appreciated by French people when guests try to speak their language. It's also important to remember that not all signs or directions in Bordeaux will include an English translation, even if many menus will. When you're traveling around the city and visiting less visited places, it can be helpful to have a pocket dictionary or a translation app.

Although most waiters in restaurants speak English, it's courteous to begin in French and transition to English as necessary. Additionally, as English might not be as frequently understood in rural or isolated places close to Bordeaux, it's beneficial to acquire a little bit of French.

12.2 Advice on Budgeting and Currency
The euro (€) is the currency used in Bordeaux and the rest of France. If you're coming from a non-euro country, it's critical to be mindful of exchange rates. The majority of currencies are exchangeable at banks, exchange offices

located throughout the city, and the airport. Although most restaurants, stores, and hotels in Bordeaux take credit and debit cards, it's still a good idea to have some cash on hand for smaller purchases, particularly at local markets, cafés, or smaller venues.

There are several ATMs in Bordeaux, and taking out cash in the local currency is frequently the most economical choice. Just make sure to inquire about any fees related to foreign withdrawals from your bank. In France, service fees are usually included in restaurant bills when it comes to tipping. However, if you are especially pleased with the service, it is traditional to offer a little tip (about 5–10%).

Bordeaux is generally thought to be reasonably priced when compared to other large French cities like Paris or Nice, though prices can change according to where you choose to eat or stay. Here are some general pointers for planning your trip's budget:

- Meals: A dinner at a budget restaurant will set you back between €15 and €25 per person. A three-course meal at a mid-range restaurant may cost between €30 and €50.

- Accommodation: Budget hotels in Bordeaux can cost as little as €60 per night, while mid-range hotels can cost as much as €150. Luxurious lodgings might cost more than €200 per night.
- Public transport: A day pass costs about €4.30, and a one-way ticket on the tram system is €1.70.

You may enjoy Bordeaux without going over your budget if you plan ahead and keep an eye on your daily spending.

12.3 Safety and Emergency Contacts
Although traveling in Bordeaux is generally safe, it's always a good idea to be ready for anything. The following are crucial emergency contacts and safety advice:

Calls for Emergencies:
Emergency Services (Police, Fire, Ambulance): In the event of an emergency, dial 112 or 18 for prompt assistance. Any mobile phone can be used to dial the European Union emergency number, which is 112.
- Medical Assistance: To contact emergency services in the event of a medical emergency, phone 112 or 15 for an ambulance.

Local Police: 17 is the number to call the local police station.

Bordeaux is home to a large number of pharmacies, some of which are open around-the-clock. Look for a green cross sign in the window to determine which pharmacies are open later.

Although Bordeaux is a relatively safe city, it's still vital to remain mindful of your surroundings, just like in any other urban setting. Pickpocketing and other forms of petty theft can happen in tourist destinations including train stations, marketplaces, and public transportation. When using your phone in public, exercise caution and always keep your possessions safe. The local police are always ready to help if you need assistance or have any concerns.

Make sure that your home country's health insurance covers international travel in case of health-related concerns. If not, think about getting medical coverage for your trip to Bordeaux with your travel insurance.

Resources and Apps for Travel
Whether you're organizing your trip or just trying to navigate your way around Bordeaux, technology can be a great help. To help you get the most out of your vacation, here are some helpful travel applications and resources:

One of the most important tools for navigating Bordeaux is Google Maps. It can assist you in locating local points of interest, walking routes, and public transportation routes. Additionally, you can utilize it to find eateries, stores, and other establishments when exploring other districts.

Trams, buses, and ferries in Bordeaux can be found with the help of TBM Bordeaux, the official app for the city's public transportation system. Planning your excursions across the city is made simple by the real-time access to schedules, route maps, and ticket alternatives.

- HappyCow: The HappyCow app provides a list of plant-based and sustainable restaurants in Bordeaux for people looking for vegetarian, vegan, or environmentally conscious dining options. To assist you in selecting the greatest locations for wholesome, eco-friendly meals, it additionally offers reviews and ratings.

The official tourism app for Bordeaux offers detailed information about the city's events, restaurants, attractions, and more. It's a useful tool for organizing your schedule and learning about the events taking place in Bordeaux while you're there.

- XE Currency: XE Currency is a user-friendly program that can assist you in converting your local currency to euros depending on exchange rates. Travelers who wish to monitor the currency rate and steer clear of needless costs may find this very helpful.

Having these tools at your disposal guarantees that you're always informed, which will facilitate and enhance your trip to Bordeaux. These useful resources will help you stay organized and connected whether you're budgeting, traversing the city, or seeking emergency assistance.

You can travel to Bordeaux with confidence if you keep these useful pointers in mind, knowing that you'll be able to take care of everything. Having the correct information can help you make the most of your time in this stunning city, whether it be with communication, budgeting, safety, or digital tools. Have fun while you're traveling!

BORDEAUX FOR DIFFERENT TRAVELERS

No matter who you are or what kind of experience you're looking for, Bordeaux is a city that embraces everyone. Bordeaux has something to offer everyone, whether you're traveling with family, seeking a romantic getaway, exploring alone, or need accessible options. In order to make your trip comfortable, pleasurable, and unforgettable, this section will highlight the top travel-related activities and advice for various kinds of tourists.

Activities That Are Family-Friendly
Bordeaux offers a variety of family-friendly activities that will keep the little ones occupied and entertained, even though traveling with kids may occasionally be difficult. Bordeaux provides a friendly atmosphere for families, whether they want to visit the city's parks, museums, or engage in interactive activities.

The Jardin Public, a sizable green park with playgrounds, a lovely lake, and lots of room for outdoor games and picnics, is one of Bordeaux's most well-liked family attractions.

Kids can also take a ride on the park's miniature train, which is a fun activity for them. The park is the ideal location for your kids to run around and take in the fresh air because of its laid-back vibe.

A must-see for families with little children is the Cap Sciences museum. A range of hands-on displays are available at this interactive science museum to stimulate young minds and promote learning via play. Children will be captivated by the museum's displays and relish the chance to experiment and learn, whether they are investigating the realms of sound, motion, or light.

A fantastic family-friendly visit is the wine museum, La Cité du Vin. Although the museum is primarily intended for adults, family packages are available, and kids may take advantage of the immersive experiences that highlight the history and culture of Bordeaux winemaking. With serene waters and breathtaking vistas, a boat trip on the Garonne River is a great option for those seeking a more outdoor experience to experience the city from a new angle.

Bordeaux has family-friendly dining alternatives to satisfy everyone. In order to accommodate families, several restaurants offer flexible seating arrangements or children's menus. Delicious meals for all ages are served at Le Mably, a laid-back and cozy restaurant in the center of Bordeaux that makes sure everyone is satisfied.

Romantic Vacations
For couples looking for a romantic retreat, Bordeaux is the ideal location. The city provides plenty of chances for couples to spend quality time together because of its gorgeous streets, quaint cafés, and well-known wine culture.

Explore Bordeaux's Old Town and its cobbled streets to begin your romantic journey. The picturesque squares and old buildings provide the ideal setting for a leisurely stroll. Enjoy a bottle of Bordeaux wine or a cup of coffee at a café at Place des Quinconces and just spend time together. Another well-known romantic location in Bordeaux is the Place de la Bourse, which has a mirrored water mirror. It is particularly lovely at sunset when the sky turns golden and the water's reflections sparkle.

Reserve a wine-tasting trip at one of the neighboring vineyards for a more exclusive experience. Bordeaux is the world's wine capital, and you and your significant other may enjoy world-class wines while discovering the history and culture of winemaking by touring the neighboring wine area. Just outside of Bordeaux, the quaint medieval village of Saint-Émilion provides romantic wine tours that include private tastings and breathtaking views of the undulating hills.

Take a hot air balloon ride over the area if you want something more unusual. Together with the peaceful calm of the balloon, the view of the vineyards, rivers, and undulating countryside below you makes for a genuinely romantic and unique experience.

Bordeaux comes alive with romantic supper options in the evening. Enjoy Michelin-starred French cuisine at the city's many upscale eating establishments, including Le Pressoir d'Argent. As an alternative, La Brasserie de la Lune provides a more relaxed yet cozy setting ideal for sharing a delectable lunch.

Advice for Traveling Alone

Bordeaux provides a friendly atmosphere for lone visitors, allowing them to explore at their own leisure. Whether you are a history enthusiast, art lover, or just trying to decompress, there are many things to explore alone in this somewhat easy-to-navigate city.

Visit the Musée des Beaux-Arts to begin your solo journey and become fully immersed in Bordeaux's rich artistic past. The museum is serene, and looking through its sculptures and paintings is a calming and motivating experience. After that, go along the Garonne River, where you'll find picturesque locations and seats ideal for admiring the scenery and thinking back on your visit.

The opportunity to freely explore Bordeaux's lively markets will also be appreciated by lone visitors. A variety of locally grown, fresh produce, cheeses, meats, and handcrafted crafts are available at the Marché des Capucins. Enjoy a light supper at one of the market's cafés or pick up some fresh supplies for a picnic while strolling about and learning about the local way of life.

If you're seeking a chance to meet other tourists, the city has a number of hostels and common areas where you can meet others who share your interests. Numerous neighborhood cafés and coworking spaces provide welcoming environments where lone travelers can unwind, read, or work while enjoying the city's views and sounds. Darwin is a hip café and coworking space that's perfect for meeting locals and other tourists in a relaxed, artistic setting.

Bordeaux is also a fantastic place for dining alone because so many restaurants provide modest tables or single sitting. Enjoy a meal at Le Bistrot du Gabriel, which has a friendly ambiance and great French food, or have dinner by yourself at one of Bordeaux's many wine bars, where you can sip on some of the region's best wine.

Bordeaux Is Accessible
Bordeaux is making efforts to make the city accessible to everyone, including those with mobility impairments. The majority of trams and buses in the city have wheelchair and stroller places, making the public transportation system wheelchair accessible. Many hotels offer accommodations for visitors

with disabilities, such as handrails, easy-access showers, and other essential features.

With their smooth walkways and convenient seats, the Place de la Bourse and Le Miroir d'Eau are both accessible to people with mobility impairments. With accessible walkways in many of Bordeaux's parks, such as Parc Bordelais, it's simple to enjoy the outdoors without worrying about obstacles.

Vélo Bordeaux Métropole provides a selection of accessible bikes for visitors with wheelchairs or scooters, enabling them to move through the city at their own speed. The city offers river cruises, which offer a tranquil way to view the city from the water, if you would rather not ride a bicycle.

Bordeaux offers a number of services for disabled travelers who need medical assistance or unique accommodations. A great place to look for accessible lodging, sights, and transportation is the Bordeaux Tourist Office.

Bordeaux is a city that welcomes all kinds of tourists, regardless of why they are there. Couples can spend romantic moments in the city's most picturesque locations, families will find plenty of activities to keep kids busy, single visitors can take their time exploring, and people with mobility impairments can feel secure knowing Bordeaux provides accessible options to make their trip enjoyable. Bordeaux makes sure that every visitor may have an amazing time with well-considered lodging, a variety of activities, and a friendly atmosphere.

SEASONAL HIGHLIGHTS

Bordeaux is a city that provides year-round unique experiences because of its breathtaking scenery and rich cultural legacy. Bordeaux presents itself differently depending on the season, whether you're organizing a winter retreat or a spring vacation. Every season offers fresh pleasures and exploration opportunities, from the busy summer to the serene fall. The finest times to visit, the city's seasonal changes, and the must-attend special events in 2025 are all highlighted in this section.

The Ideal Time to Go
Bordeaux has something unique to offer in every season, so the ideal time to visit really depends on your tastes. Spring (March to May) is the best season to go if you want moderate weather, less crowds, and a more laid-back vibe. Comfortable temperatures prevail, and the city's vineyards and gardens begin to bloom, releasing fragrant, new flowers into the air. The wine season begins in the spring, so it's a great opportunity to see the nearby vineyards before harvest takes over.

Summer (June to August) is the most energetic time of year to visit Bordeaux if you want pleasant weather and a bustling environment. There are lots of options for wine tours, river cruises, and leisurely walks along the riverbanks during the long, sunny days, and the city comes alive with outdoor events, festivals, and activities. But summer can also be the busiest time of year, so be ready for a more crowded setting and more expensive lodging.

Another fantastic season to visit is **Autumn (September to November)**, especially for wine enthusiasts. The city is filled with enthusiasm and anticipation as the grape harvest season approaches, and the weather stays pleasant. Fall is a photographer's dream since it gives the surrounding landscape and vineyards a golden tint. Life slows down, giving you more time to enjoy Bordeaux at your own speed.

Winter (December to February) is the time to go if you want to be more peaceful and reflective. You may tour Bordeaux's museums, galleries, and cafés without the typical bustle because the crowds have subsided. Bordeaux rarely experiences snow, even if temperatures might drop, and the city's markets and holiday lights add a unique touch to the winter season. Bordeaux has a certain allure in the winter if you enjoy snug times and more subdued views.

The Seasons of Bordeaux
Every season in Bordeaux offers a fresh viewpoint on the city, highlighting various facets of its culture and beauty.

Spring (March to May) – Bordeaux's spring is a season of rebirth as the city emerges from winter. As flowers blossom, the parks and gardens, such as Parc Bordelais and Jardin Public, come alive with color, providing a serene setting for picnics or leisurely walks. The pleasant weather makes it ideal for touring Bordeaux's old buildings and cobblestone streets. Spring is an excellent time to go on a vineyard tour, when you can observe the vines beginning to develop in preparation for the summer harvest, as the city's vineyards start to come alive with activity. The Bordeaux Wine Festival, a must-attend occasion for wine lovers, is also taking place this season.

Summer (June to August) - Bordeaux's lively vitality is evident in the summer months. Cafés line the pavements, the streets are bustling with activity, and there are countless chances for outdoor adventures throughout the long, bright days. Near Place de la Bourse, the Miroir d'Eau reflects the summer sky brilliantly, making it an ideal location for photographs. Bordeaux holds a number of cultural events at this period, such as the Fête de la Musique in June, when musicians throng the streets, and Les Epicuriales, a food and wine festival honoring the best cuisine in the area. The refreshing wind of summer evenings makes it the perfect season to take in Bordeaux's exciting nightlife or savor outdoor dining by the Garonne River.

Autumn (September to November) Bordeaux's fall season is enchanting, particularly for wine enthusiasts. Bordeaux is surrounded by a landscape of gold and crimson when the grape harvest starts in September. Because you may sample some of the best Bordeaux wines and take in the harvest atmosphere, the lower temps are ideal for wine excursions. Additionally, there are fewer tourists in the fall, so things move more slowly. The birthplace of Montesquieu, the Château de la Brède, is especially beautiful in the fall, when the surrounding gardens and forests are glowing with the changing of the seasons. It's a fantastic time to enjoy robust French cuisine because the local farmers' markets are brimming with fresh food.

Winter (December–February) — Bordeaux has a more subdued, private vibe in the winter. The city's historic buildings are illuminated by the joyous holiday lights, which create a cozy and inviting ambiance. Bordeaux hosts its Christmas markets throughout the winter, where you can buy handcrafted gifts, sip mulled wine, and savor seasonal fare like gingerbread and roasted chestnuts. Bordeaux rarely has snowfall, so even if the weather can be cold, it's ideal for strolling about the city's galleries, museums, and stores. Because there won't be as many people there, you'll have more room to enjoy Bordeaux's architectural and cultural landmarks, such the Place des Quinconces and the Musée d'Art Contemporain.

Holidays and Special Occasions in 2025
Bordeaux's calendar is jam-packed with fascinating events that showcase the city's rich history, culture, and love of wine. These 2025 holidays and special events will add even more significance to your trip.

One of the city's most recognizable events is the Bordeaux Wine Festival (June 2025), which takes place every two years. Winemakers from all throughout the region come together for this four-day celebration of Bordeaux's rich wine legacy. While learning about the origins and production methods of Bordeaux's well-known wines, visitors can partake in food pairings, vineyard excursions, and tastings. In addition, the festival offers wine seminars, live music, and even boat cruises on the Garonne River, where you can sip wine and take in the breathtaking scenery.

The Fête de la Musique (June 2025) is a music festival that brings live performers to Bordeaux's parks, squares, and streets. Musicians of different genres use the city as a stage, performing everything from jazz and classical to rock and electronic. You're bound to come across a live performance that heightens the celebratory ambiance, whether you're lounging in a café or exploring the Jardin Public.

Les Epicuriales (May-June 2025) - This festival is a must-attend for everyone who enjoys gastronomy. With dozens of outstanding chefs showcasing their best creations in a lively outdoor setting, this event honors Bordeaux's culinary prowess. Visitors from all over the world come to celebrate the local produce, wine, and cuisine. Bordeaux's finest cuisine, including foie gras and fresh oysters, will be available for you to try during this time, along with superb regional wines.

- Christmas Markets (December 2025) - With their festive decorations, sparkling lights, and stalls offering handcrafted items, regional produce, and seasonal treats, Bordeaux's Christmas markets are a mystical experience. It's the ideal time to visit for a warm, Christmas escape because the city's historic core is turned into a winter wonderland.

From the lively summer festivals to the serene allure of winter, Bordeaux's seasonal highlights have plenty to offer all types of tourists. The city's culture, beauty, and world-class wine will make your visit unforgettable at any time. Bordeaux is a city that welcomes you to experience it in all seasons, whether you like the vibrant energy of summer or the serene atmosphere of autumn.

FINAL TIPS AND INSIGHTS

In order to make your vacation to Bordeaux seamless, pleasurable, and unforgettable, here are some last-minute pointers and advice. To help you feel well-prepared before your trip, we'll go over typical blunders to avoid, local etiquette and customs, and answers to some commonly asked questions in this part.

Typical Errors to Steer Clear of

Although Bordeaux is a friendly city, first-time visitors frequently make a few basic blunders that are easily avoided with a little planning.

1. Not scheduling wine tours ahead of time – A highlight of any trip to Bordeaux, the world's wine capital, is taking a vineyard tour. But wine tastings and tours may fill up fast, particularly in the spring and fall when demand is highest. It's best to schedule your vineyard excursions in advance to ensure you have the experience you desire. This is especially crucial for well-known and sometimes in-demand wineries in neighboring regions like Saint-Émilion or Pomerol.

2. Ignoring the necessity of restaurant reservations – Even while Bordeaux offers a lot of great places to eat, especially in the city center, it's vital to remember that many of the more well-known eateries require reservations, especially on weekends or in the evenings. Walk-in customers might not be able to eat at their preferred time or might have to wait for a table. Make reservations at least a day or two in advance to minimize disappointment, particularly if you intend to eat at upscale restaurants.

3. Ignoring the museums' and attractions' opening hours – The museums and galleries in Bordeaux, like those in many other European towns, have set hours of operation; some may be closed on Mondays or during lunch. To make sure you don't miss any must-see sites, it's a good idea to confirm the hours before leaving. Additionally, certain attractions can be closed completely or have shortened hours during the off-season, so make plans in advance to avoid any surprises.

Using ridesharing services or taxis excessively 4. Public transportation is the fastest and most convenient method to get around Bordeaux, and it has a great system. Bicycles, buses, and trams are all easily accessible and can take you to the majority of the city's main attractions. Over-reliance on ridesharing or taxis can be costly and may not always be the best option for getting around the city, particularly during rush hour.

5. Not sampling enough regional food - Bordeaux is renowned for its delicious food, and if you're pressed for time, it's simple to stick to tried-and-true selections. But be sure to sample some of the local specialties, such as oysters from the Arcachon Bay, canelés (caramelized custard cakes), and magret de canard (duck breast). These regional specialties are worth the indulgence and are essential to Bordeaux's identity.

Customs & Etiquette in the Area

Like most of France, Bordeaux has its own set of social mores and manners. You can feel more at ease and guarantee that you leave a good impression on the locals by being aware of these.

1. Saying "Bonjour" with grace – A simple "Bonjour" (good day) or "Bonsoir" (good

evening) is required when entering stores, restaurants, or other facilities in Bordeaux, and throughout France. It is respectful to greet people before starting a discussion; otherwise, it could come out as rude.

2. Etiquette in Dining – Keep in mind that lunches in Bordeaux are usually unhurried affairs. Locals typically eat slowly, especially during lunch, which can go on for an hour or longer. A sit-down lunch is an opportunity to enjoy the food and the atmosphere, so don't expect a speedy meal. Furthermore, since service fees are covered by the bill in France, tipping is not required. However, for excellent service, it is appreciated if you round up the amount or leave a little tip (5–10%).

3. The dress code Bordeaux is less formal than Paris, yet the French are generally appreciative of a polished appearance. Dressing nicely is a fantastic idea while going to fancy restaurants, theaters, or wine bars. For the majority of activities, comfortable yet fashionable attire is ideal; however, if you intend to visit upscale venues, a more formal appearance is recommended.

Smoking in public areas 4. Although there are approved smoking sites, smoking is nevertheless quite common in Bordeaux, especially outside. It is forbidden to smoke in enclosed public areas like restaurants, museums, and public transportation. Because residents are often considerate of smoking sites, be careful where you light up.

5. Being on time - Even though the French have a reputation for being carefree with time, formal occasions and corporate environments nevertheless appreciate punctuality. Being punctual is polite when you're meeting someone for dinner or an appointment. However, it's normally okay to arrive 15 to 20 minutes later than the allocated time if you've been invited to a social event or supper with friends.

Common Questions and Answers

The answers to some of the most common queries tourists have about Bordeaux will help you make the most of your trip.

Q1: Can you stroll around Bordeaux?
Yes, it's extremely easy to walk around Bordeaux. It is simple to explore the historic

center on foot because it is small and pedestrian-friendly. You can stroll to many of the city's major attractions, such as parks, museums, and dining establishments. Public transportation is also easily accessible if you choose to continue your exploration.

Q2: Is proficiency in French required to travel to Bordeaux?
Although Bordeaux's official language is French, many residents speak at least some English, particularly in tourist destinations including dining establishments, lodging facilities, and tourist attractions. Nevertheless, it is always appreciated when guests try to say a few phrases in French, such as "merci" (thank you) and "bonjour" (hello). Making a good impression starts with simple greetings and words.

Q3: Is it simple to get to the wine regions from Bordeaux?
Bordeaux is in a good position to visit neighboring wine areas such as Saint-Émilion, Médoc, and Pomerol. From the city, day trips are simple to arrange by bus, train, or even rental car. Visitors can easily explore the wine country with the help of numerous wine tours

that depart from Bordeaux and provide guided tours to the greatest vineyards in the area.

Q4: How can one navigate Bordeaux most effectively?

Trams, buses, and bicycles are all part of Bordeaux's effective and reasonably priced public transportation network. For quick excursions throughout the city, you can rent bikes through the Vélo Bordeaux Métropole bike-sharing program, which is very well-liked. The historic core can also be explored on foot, and if necessary, there are taxis and ridesharing services like Uber available.

Q5: Does Bordeaux have any food markets?
Yes, there are a number of excellent food markets in Bordeaux. The largest and most well-known market in the city, the Marché des Capucins, sells artisanal goods, meats, cheeses, and fresh produce. It's the ideal location to experience the cuisine of the area and try some of the local specialties.

You may get the most out of your vacation to Bordeaux by remembering these last pointers and advice. These pointers will help you feel secure and prepared to take advantage of everything this lovely city has to offer, whether you're navigating the city's etiquette, avoiding typical blunders, or just being ready for what's ahead.

APPENDIX

In this section, you'll find essential resources to enhance your experience in Bordeaux and ensure a smooth and enjoyable visit. Whether you're looking for detailed maps of the city, useful French phrases to help navigate conversations, or further reading on Bordeaux's history and culture, this appendix has you covered. These tools will provide clarity and convenience, allowing you to make the most of your time in Bordeaux.

Maps of Bordeaux and Surrounding Areas

Having access to a reliable map is one of the best ways to navigate Bordeaux, whether you're strolling through its charming streets, exploring vineyards outside the city, or finding your way to a new restaurant. Here are the key maps and resources you should have:

- City Map of Bordeaux: A city map is crucial for locating main attractions, transport links, and neighborhoods in Bordeaux. It will help you find places like Place de la Bourse, Le Miroir d'Eau, and the Garonne River, ensuring you don't miss any iconic sights. This map is readily available at tourist offices or can be downloaded online through various apps or websites.

- Public Transport Map: Bordeaux's public transport system is comprehensive, and having a map of the tram and bus lines will make your travel more efficient. The TBM (Transports Bordeaux Métropole) network operates a system of trams, buses, and ferries. A map of the system can be downloaded from their website, or you can pick up a paper version at tram stations and the tourist office.

- Bordeaux Wine Region Map: If you're planning to visit the vineyards surrounding Bordeaux, a specialized map of the wine regions such as Médoc, Saint-Émilion, and Graves will help you navigate the diverse wine routes. These maps often highlight recommended routes for wine tours, where you'll find the most renowned vineyards and châteaux.

- Walking Tours and Historical Sites Map: Bordeaux's rich history is reflected in its beautiful architecture and landmarks. A walking tour map is perfect for a self-guided exploration of historical sites, such as La Cité du Vin, Bordeaux's Old Town, and Place des Quinconces. These maps often provide helpful details about the best walking routes, distances, and the most significant historical buildings to explore.

Glossary of French Terms for Travelers

Although Bordeaux is a popular tourist destination and many locals speak some English, knowing a few key French phrases can enhance your experience and interactions with locals. Here's a glossary of essential French terms that can help you navigate everyday situations while in Bordeaux:

- Bonjour (bohn-zhoor) – Hello / Good morning
- Bonsoir (bohn-swahr) – Good evening
- Merci (mehr-see) – Thank you
- S'il vous plaît (seel voo pleh) – Please
- Excusez-moi (ehk-skew-zay mwah) – Excuse me
- Parlez-vous anglais ? (par-lay voo ahn-glay?) – Do you speak English?
- Où est... ? (oo eh) – Where is...?
- Combien ça coûte ? (kohm-byen sah koot?) – How much does it cost?

- L'addition, s'il vous plaît (la-dee-syon seel voo pleh) – The bill, please
- Un café, s'il vous plaît (uhn kah-fay seel voo pleh) – A coffee, please
- Je voudrais... (zhuh voo-dray) – I would like...
- Où sont les toilettes ? (oo sohn lay twah-let?) – Where are the toilets?
- Aidez-moi (eh-day mwah) – Help me
- C'est délicieux ! (say day-lee-syu) – It's delicious!
- Fermé (fair-may) – Closed
- Ouvert (oo-ver) – Open
- Comment ça va ? (koh-mohn sah vah?) – How are you?
- Très bien, merci. (tray byan mehr-see) – Very well, thank you.

By learning these simple phrases, you'll be able to communicate more easily with locals and show respect for their language and culture. While English is spoken at many tourist spots, using even a little French can go a long way in making connections and enjoying your trip more fully.

Additional Reading and Resources

For those looking to deepen their knowledge of Bordeaux before or after their trip, a range of books, websites, and other resources can provide valuable insights into the city's history, culture, and culinary scene.

- Books on Bordeaux:
  - Bordeaux: The Wine Region by Michel Dovaz – A comprehensive guide to the wine-producing region of Bordeaux, this book explores the history of Bordeaux's vineyards, wine production techniques, and the best wine routes to explore.
  - The Bordeaux Companion by Robert M. Parker Jr. – This book is perfect for wine enthusiasts. It offers an in-depth look at Bordeaux's wine, including the best vineyards, wine-tasting tours, and tips for navigating the region's wines.
  - Bordeaux: A Cultural and Culinary Journey by Mary Ellen O'Connell – This beautifully written book delves into the cultural history of Bordeaux and provides an immersive experience into the city's food scene, offering culinary tours and stories that will make any visitor feel connected to the heart of Bordeaux.

- Websites:
  - Tourism Bordeaux: Bordeaux's official tourism website offers a wealth of information, including detailed guides to the city's attractions, events, accommodations, and more. It's a great resource for current events, tips, and recommendations.

-Website: www.bordeaux-tourism.co.uk
  - La Cité du Vin: A must-visit for wine lovers, this site offers detailed information about Bordeaux's wine museum, upcoming events, and exhibits related to the history and culture of wine.

-Website: www.laciteduvin.com
  - Bordeaux Wine Routes: If you're planning a wine tour in the surrounding vineyards, this website offers in-depth guides to the wine regions of Bordeaux, providing recommendations for wineries, wine festivals, and more.

-Website: www.bordeaux-wine-routes.com

- Apps:
  - Citymapper: This app is great for navigating Bordeaux's public transportation system, including trams, buses, and cycling routes. It provides real-time updates on transport options and routes, helping you get around the city efficiently.
  - Vélo Bordeaux Métropole: If you prefer cycling, this app lets you easily rent and return bikes across the city. It shows available bikes, bike stations, and provides route suggestions for cycling tours.
  - Tripadvisor: For restaurant reviews, activity recommendations, and hotel booking options, Tripadvisor remains one of the most reliable resources for travelers. You can also read reviews from other travelers and plan your itinerary accordingly.

With these maps, phrases, and additional resources, you'll be equipped to make your trip to Bordeaux as enjoyable and seamless as possible. From navigating the city with ease to deepening your knowledge of its history and culture, these tools ensure that you'll have everything you need to make the most of your time in this beautiful, historic city.

Printed in Great Britain
by Amazon